D0554794

Aloian, Molly.
How do we know it is
fall? /
c2013.
33305229080365
sa   06/23/14

we know it is
Fall?

Molly Aloian

Crabtree Publishing Company
www.crabtreebooks.com

Author
Molly Aloian

Publishing plan research and development
Sean Charlebois, Reagan Miller
Crabtree Publishing Company

Editorial director
Kathy Middleton

Editors
Adrianna Morganelli
Crystal Sikkens

Photo research and design
Margaret Amy Salter

**Production coordinator
and prepress technician**
Margaret Amy Salter

Print coordinator
Katherine Berti

Illustrations
Katherine Berti: page 6

Photographs
Thinkstock: cover (middle), top border, pages 1, 5, 7, 10,
   12, 13, 14, 15, (ash & right), 16, 17, 18, 19, 22 (camera)
Shutterstock: cover (top and bottom), pages 4, 8, 9, 11,
   15 (except ash and right), 20, 21, 22 (except camera)

Library and Archives Canada Cataloguing in Publication

Aloian, Molly
     How do we know it is fall? / Molly Aloian.

(Seasons close-up)
Includes index.
Issued also in electronic formats.
ISBN 978-0-7787-0961-9 (bound).--ISBN 978-0-7787-0965-7 (pbk.)

     1. Autumn--Juvenile literature. 2. Seasons--Juvenile literature.
I. Title. II. Series: Seasons close-up

QB637.7.A56 2013   j508.2   C2012-907352-0

Library of Congress Cataloging-in-Publication Data

CIP available at Library of Congress

Crabtree Publishing Company

Printed in Canada/102013/MA20130906

www.crabtreebooks.com   1-800-387-7650

Copyright © **2013 CRABTREE PUBLISHING COMPANY.** All rights reserved. No part of this publication may be reproduced, stored in a retrieval system or be transmitted in any form or by any means, electronic, mechanical, photocopying, recording, or otherwise, without the prior written permission of Crabtree Publishing Company. In Canada: We acknowledge the financial support of the Government of Canada through the Canada Book Fund for our publishing activities.

Published in Canada
Crabtree Publishing
616 Welland Ave.
St. Catharines, Ontario
L2M 5V6

Published in the United States
Crabtree Publishing
PMB 59051
350 Fifth Avenue, 59th Floor
New York, New York 10118

Published in the United Kingdom
Crabtree Publishing
Maritime House
Basin Road North, Hove
BN41 1WR

Published in Australia
Crabtree Publishing
3 Charles Street
Coburg North
VIC 3058

Contents

What is fall?

Most places on Earth have four **seasons** that follow the same pattern each year. The pattern always repeats in the same way: winter—spring—summer—fall—winter. Fall always comes after summer and before winter. In some places, fall is called autumn.

Fall

Spring

Summer

Winter

Cooler weather

Cooler weather is a sign that fall has arrived. The land, air, and water are still warm from all the summer sunshine, but the temperatures are cooler during fall. The weather can also change often. Some days can be warm and sunny and others are cold and rainy. Some days may be stormy with strong winds.

The season fall got its name because it is the time of year when leaves fall to the ground.

Why do we have fall?

It takes Earth one year, or 12 months, to travel once around the Sun. As its moving, Earth is spinning on a tilted **axis**. Because of this, parts of Earth get different amounts of sunlight at different times of the year. The different amounts of sunlight make each season different.

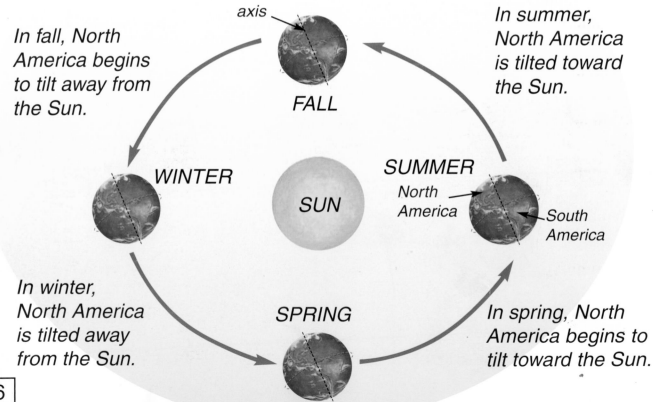

axis

In fall, North America begins to tilt away from the Sun.

FALL

In summer, North America is tilted toward the Sun.

WINTER

SUMMER

SUN

North America

South America

In winter, North America is tilted away from the Sun.

SPRING

In spring, North America begins to tilt toward the Sun.

Tilting away

During fall in North America, the northern parts of Earth begin to tilt away from the Sun. This means North America is receiving less sunlight. Less sunlight brings cooler temperatures and shorter amounts of daylight.

Warm days and cool nights are signs that fall has arrived. What are some other signs of fall?

What do you think?

In what season is it darkest, and in what season is it lightest? Why do you think this is?

When is fall?

All the seasons, including fall, last for three months.
In North America, the first day of fall is in September.
In the southern parts of Earth, however, the seasons
are opposite. So when fall is starting in North America,
spring is beginning in South America.

Fall in South America begins in March.

Parts of Africa have two seasons. During the rainy season, roads can get flooded.

Two instead of four

Certain parts of the world do not have fall. In these places they only have two seasons: the rainy season and the dry season. During the rainy season, there is heavy rain. During the dry season, there is very little rain.

9

Big changes

Summer is a bright, sunny season. During summer, plants are growing and flowering and there are animals everywhere. Fall is a colder, quieter season. Long, hot summer days gradually become shorter and cooler.

During fall, the green leaves on trees begin to turn various colors of red, yellow, and orange.

Getting prepared

In summer, you see plenty of birds and hear them chirping and singing. Insects, such as bees and butterflies, fly from plant to plant. During fall, birds become quieter and many insects and other animals starting looking for shelter for the cold winter. Some animals may also leave for warmer places.

This chipmunk is collecting leaves to make a warm nest for the winter.

Fall weather

During fall, the weather is usually warm, but not hot. The Sun may feel warm, but the wind can be chilly and temperatures often drop at night. Many people wear sweaters or light jackets if they go outdoors on a fall day.

What do you think?

What three things do you like about fall? What three things do you dislike about fall?

Hurricanes can cause a lot of damage.

Storms, fog, and frost

During fall, there are sometimes violent storms called hurricanes. Hurricanes are storms with strong spinning winds and heavy rain. There may also be **fog** and **frost** during fall.

Frost means the end of the growing season for many plants.

Plants in fall

In fall, there are fewer hours of daylight. Days get shorter and nights become longer. Less daylight means that plants slowly stop growing. The green leaves on trees change color. They turn beautiful shades of brown, orange, yellow, and red. Then they die and fall to the ground.

Many maples

The leaves of oak, poplar, ash, and birch trees all change color during fall. Maple trees are some of the most colorful fall trees. There are more than 100 **species**, or types, of maple trees.

Oak

Poplar

Ash

Birch

Maple

As winter approaches, maple trees lose their leaves to prepare for the winter.

Animals in fall

Honeybees

During summer, there is plenty of food for animals and their babies. Once fall arrives, there is less food. Many animals begin storing food in fall in order to prepare for the cold winter. Squirrels and chipmunks collect nuts and seeds and bury them underground. Honeybees store honey in their **hives**.

Hibernate and migrate

Some animals, such as raccoons and bears, eat as much as they can during fall. Then they begin searching for places to **hibernate**, or go into a deep sleep, for the winter. Other animals, such as birds, get ready to **migrate**, or move to warmer places.

Raccoon

Bear

Geese

What do you think?

Name three animals that you might see in the woods on a fall day.

17

Fall fun

After the heat of summer, it is fun to play outside on a cool fall day. Many people go on hikes or nature walks in forests or parks. Raking and playing in fallen leaves is a fun way to spend a fall day.

What do you think?

Think of your favorite fall activity. What kind of clothes do you wear for the activity?

Fit for fall

The weather can change quickly in fall. For example, it may be warm and sunny one hour and rainy and chilly the next hour. When going outdoors, many people dress in layers, such as a T-shirt with a warm sweater overtop. This way they are prepared for warm or cool weather.

You may also want to bring a raincoat, boots, or an umbrella when heading outdoors on a fall day.

19

Fall harvest

Farmers **harvest** their crops in fall. They harvest crops of wheat, oats, and other grains. People need wheat to make bread and other foods during the winter. Pumpkins, squash, turnips, beets, and Brussels sprouts are all ready to be picked in fall. Fall is harvest time!

Apples and pears are ready to be picked in fall.

This farmer is out late harvesting his wheat on a fall night.

Harvest moon

A harvest moon is a large, bright full moon that occurs in fall in the northern parts of Earth. This moon comes in handy for the farmers who are working late into the night harvesting crops. The light of the harvest moon helps farmers to see while they work.

What do you think?

During fall, you might need an extra blanket on your bed. What other ways do we prepare for chilly fall nights?

Tree time

This activity will let you track the many changes that trees go through during fall. For several weeks, record what you see happening to trees and discuss the changes with your friends. You will need:

In September, choose a tree in your yard, neighborhood, park, or other area and look closely at it. Take a picture of the tree and describe it in your journal. Each week, take a new picture of the tree and describe any changes in your journal. Answer the following questions: How has the tree changed?

What animals are in the tree?

What is happening to the tree's leaves and why?

What do you think happens to the leaves that fall on the ground?

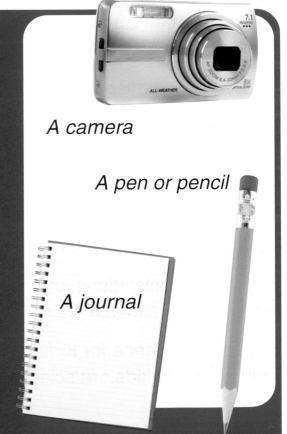

A camera

A pen or pencil

A journal

Learning more

Books

Collinson, Clare. *Fall* (Thinking About the Seasons).
Sea-to-Sea Publications, 2011.

Johnson, Robin. *What Is Weather?* (Weather Close-Up).
Crabtree Publishing Company, 2012.

Kalman, Bobbie. *Which Season Is It?* (My World).
Crabtree Publishing Company, 2011.

Rustad, Martha E.H. & Enright, Amanda. *Fall Harvests: Bringing in Food*
(Cloverleaf Books: Fall's Here!). Millbrook Press, 2011.

Websites

Changing Seasons—Exploring Nature Educational Resource
www.exploringnature.org/db/detail.php?dbID=112&detID=2634

Autumn Kids
www.treetures.com/Autumn2.html

Science projects: ideas, topics, methods, and examples
www.sciencemadesimple.com/

Seasons—Science for Kids!
www.historyforkids.org/scienceforkids/physics/weather/seasons.htm

Words to know

axis (AK-sis) noun The straight line around which Earth rotates

fog (fawg) noun A fine mist that floats in the air

frost (frawst) noun A thin layer of tiny ice crystals

harvest (HAHR-vist) verb To gather or collect a crop

hibernate (HI-ber-neyt) verb To go through winter in a sleeping or resting state

hive (hahyv) noun A home for bees

migrate (MAHY-greyt) verb Moving from one place to another for warmer weather or food

season (SEE-zuhn) noun A period of time with certain temperatures and weather

species (SPEE-sheez) adjective Types or kinds of animals with similar qualities

A *noun* is a person, place, or thing.
A *verb* is an action word that tells you what someone or something does.
An *adjective* is a word that tells you what something is like.

Index